LOVE & LEGACY

A MOTHER'S MEMOIR
CARRIED IN MY HEART

Atosha Logan

LOVE & LEGACY

A MOTHER'S MEMOIR
CARRIED IN MY HEART

Atosha Logan

COPYRIGHT © 2025 BY ATOSHA LOGAN

ALL RIGHTS RESERVED. NO PART OF THIS PUBLICATION MAY BE REPRODUCED, DISTRIBUTED, OR TRANSMITTED IN ANY FORM OR BY ANY MEANS, INCLUDING PHOTOCOPYING, RECORDING, OR OTHER ELECTRONIC OR MECHANICAL METHODS, OR OTHERWISE WITHOUT THE PRIOR WRITTEN PERMISSION OF THE AUTHOR, EXCEPT IN THE CASE OF BRIEF QUOTATIONS EMBODIED IN REVIEWS, ARTICLES, OR CRITICAL WORKS.

PLEASE NOTE THAT NO PART OF THIS BOOK MAY BE USED OR REPRODUCED IN ANY MANNER FOR THE PURPOSE OF TRAINING, ARTIFICIAL INTELLIGENCE TECHNOLOGIES, OR SYSTEMS.

FOR PERMISSION REQUESTS, CONTACT THE AUTHOR AT:
ATOSHA LOGAN, AUTHOR & PUBLISHER
INFO@ATOSHALOGAN.COM
WWW.ATOSHALOGAN.COM

ISBN: 978-1-7362267-6-6 (PAPERBACK) 978-1-7362267-7-3 (E-BOOK)
FIRST EDITION

PRINTED IN THE UNITED STATES OF AMERICA

COVER DESIGN: ATOSHA LOGAN
INTERIOR LAYOUT: ATOSHA LOGAN

About the Author

Atosha Logan is a woman of faith, strength, and purpose who has dedicated more than two decades to the field of education and is an author, life coach, and consultant. Guided by her unwavering belief in God, she has poured her heart into nurturing, mentoring, and leading others with integrity and personal motivation. Her journey reflects resilience, hope, and a deep commitment to uplifting and empowering others.

Beyond her professional calling, Atosha treasures the bonds of family and the importance of legacy. She believes that life's experiences are not only meant to be lived but also shared as testimonies of God's grace. Her passion for legacy and storytelling is rooted in a belief that God's grace carries us through every season. This memoir is her gift of love, hope, and inspiration for generations to come.

She continues to live out her purpose with faith at the center, striving to leave behind a legacy of inspiration, love, and unwavering trust in God.

info@atoshalogan.com
www.atoshalogan.com

ACKNOWLEDGEMENTS

This memoir is the reflection of many hearts and hands that have touched my life, and I am deeply grateful for each one.

God has BLESSED me with a wonderful husband and three children.

To my family—you are my foundation and my greatest source of love and support. Thank you for standing beside me through every season of joy and trial, and for reminding me daily of the meaning of unconditional love. I am grateful for the wisdom you've shared and the lessons that continue to guide my journey. Each of you has left an imprint on my story that cannot be erased.

To my close friends, thank you for your laughter, encouragement, and honesty. Your presence has been a light in both the brightest and darkest moments, and your belief in me gave me the courage to keep writing.

Most of all, I give thanks to God. Without His grace, strength, and faithfulness, none of this would have been possible. Every chapter of my life is a testament to His unfailing love.

The Legacy of Jerald & Willie Mae Williams shall continue through me!
A Legacy to Live For Inc.

CARRIED IN MY HEART

This *Mother's Memoir* belongs to:

_____

DATE:

A Mother's Memoir of Love & Legacy

A Mother's Memoir
Introduction

A mother's story is more than a record of events—it is a legacy of love, sacrifice, and strength. In these pages, a mother reflects on the joys and challenges of nurturing life, offering wisdom that transcends generations. This memoir is both a tribute and a treasure, reminding readers that a mother's influence is timeless and her love, everlasting.

From the roots that anchor us to the branches that stretch toward new horizons, these pages capture both struggle and victory. Each memory serves as a reminder that while we cannot control every circumstance, we can shape the legacy we leave behind.

This memoir is more than a story—it's an invitation to reflect on your own journey, to honor the memories that shape you, and to be inspired to live with courage and hope. reminding you of where you've been, who has walked beside you, and the dreams still waiting ahead.

Open these pages, take part in the journey, and let it spark reflection, conversation, and connection in your own life with grace, gratitude, and courage.

ALL ABOUT ME (11)

FAMILY TREE (14)

BECOMING A MOTHER (17)

EARLY YEARS & MILESTONES (32)

DAILY LIFE & ROUTINES (46)

LOVE, JOY & HUMOR (60)

CHALLENGES & RESILIENCE (74)

VALUES, FAITH & CHARACTER (88)

TRADITIONS & FAMILY CULTURE (102)

WORK, TIME & BALANCE (116)

LESSONS, GUIDANCE & ADVICE (131)

LEGACY & DREAMS FOR MY CHILD (145)

LIFE'S REFLECTIONS (161)

LETTER(S) TO LOVE ONE (162)

A MOTHER'S MEMOIR OF LOVE & LEGACY

"BE YOURSELF; EVERYONE ELSE IS ALREADY TAKEN."
— OSCAR WILDE

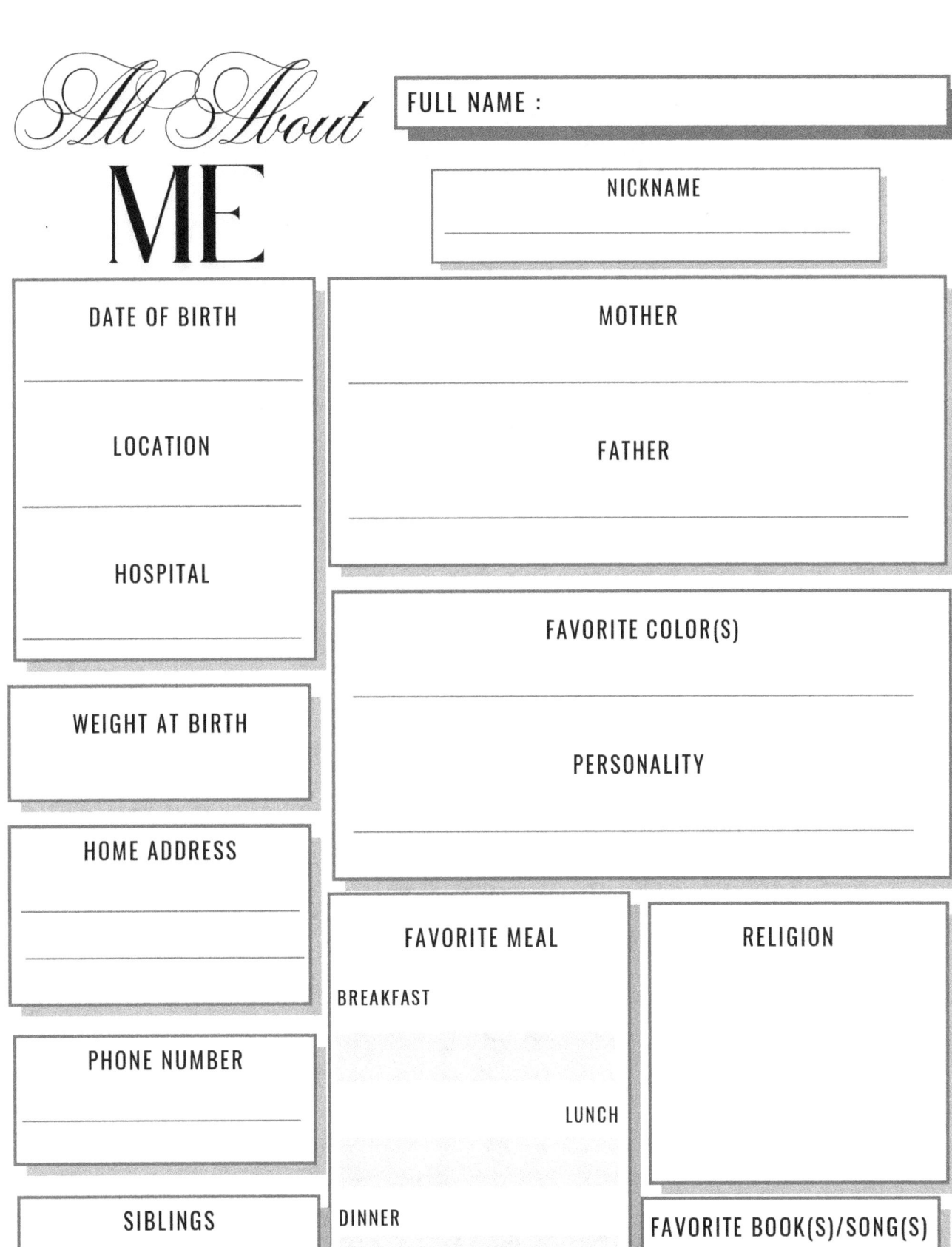

Capture the Moments

Add photos or draw pictures that represent this chapter of your life.

Memories

Memories

Memories

> "LIKE BRANCHES ON A TREE, WE ALL GROW IN DIFFERENT DIRECTIONS, YET OUR ROOTS REMAIN AS ONE."
> — ANONYMOUS

A MOTHER'S MEMOIR OF LOVE & LEGACY

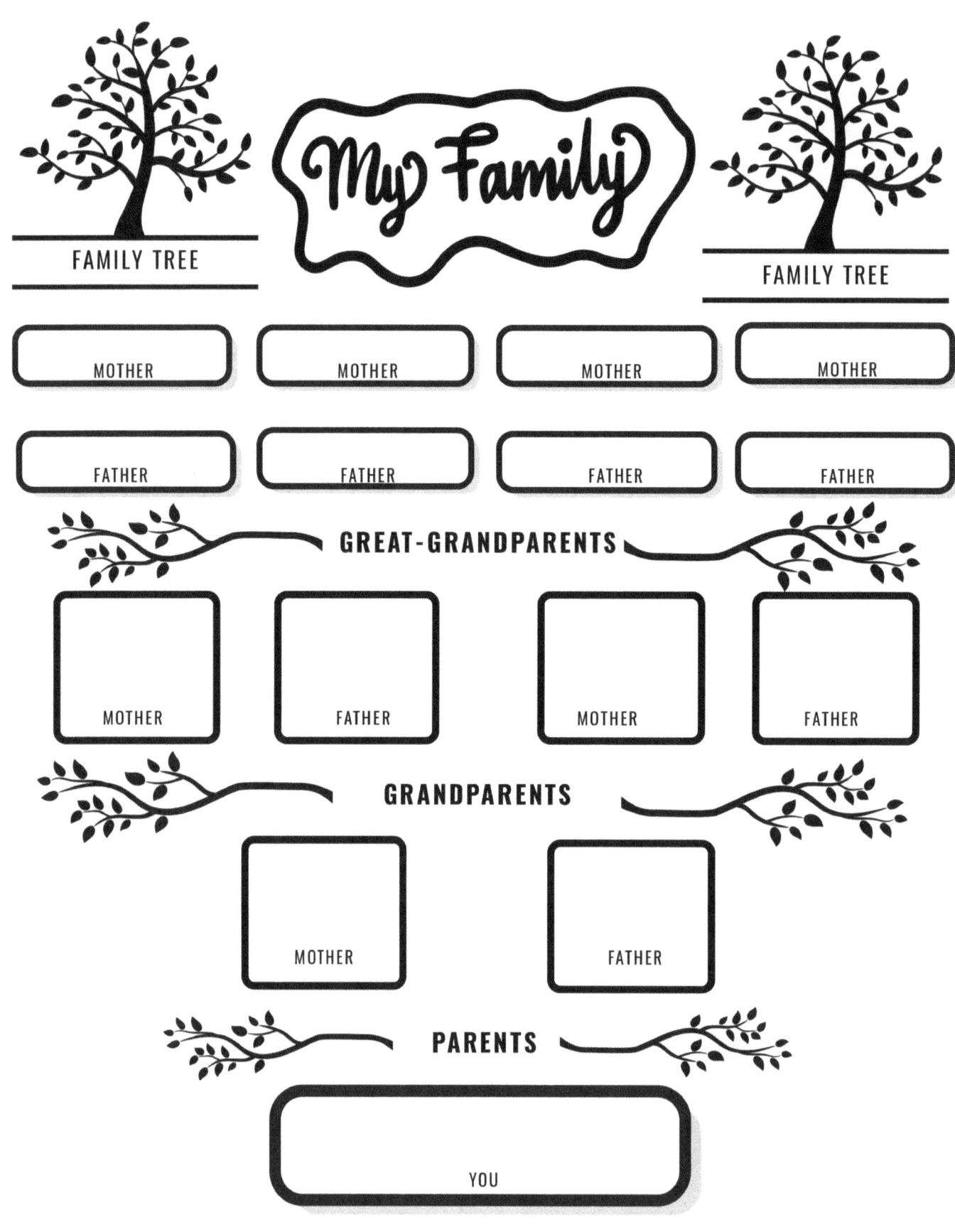

Capture the Moments
Add photos or draw pictures that represent this chapter of your life.

Memories

Memories

Memories

"THE STORIES WE LIVE BECOME THE STORIES WE LEAVE BEHIND."
— ANONYMOUS

A MOTHER'S MEMOIR OF LOVE & LEGACY

CARRIED IN MY HEART

BECOMING A MOTHER

A MOTHER'S MEMOIR OF LOVE & LEGACY

HOW DID YOU FEEL THE MOMENT
YOU LEARNED YOU WOULD BECOME A MOTHER?

WHAT DID YOU LEARN ABOUT
YOURSELF IN THOSE EARLY WEEKS AND MONTHS?

WHAT HOPES AND WORRIES CAME UP AS YOU PREPARED FOR MOTHERHOOD?

WHO DID YOU TELL FIRST?

HOW DID YOU SHARE THE NEWS?

DESCRIBE A PIECE OF ADVICE THAT HELPED YOU IN EARLY MOTHERHOOD.

WHAT SURPRISED YOU MOST ABOUT YOUR FIRST DAYS AS A MOTHER?

WHAT IMPACT HAS THIS HAD ON YOUR LIFE?

HOW DID YOUR RELATIONSHIPS WITH FAMILY AND FRIENDS SHIFT AS YOU BECAME A MOTHER?

WHAT TRADITIONS OR VALUES DID YOU DECIDE TO PASS ON FROM THE START?

HOW DID YOU MARK THE BEGINNING OF MOTHERHOOD —A RITUAL, OBJECT, OR PROMISE?

WHAT DO YOU WISH YOU COULD TELL YOUR EARLIER SELF ABOUT BECOMING A MOTHER?

additional notes

additional notes

Capture the Moments

Add photos or draw pictures that represent this chapter of your life.

Memories

Memories

Memories

> "WE DO NOT REMEMBER DAYS, WE REMEMBER MOMENTS."
> — CESARE PAVESE

A MOTHER'S MEMOIR OF LOVE & LEGACY

CARRIED IN MY HEART

EARLY DAYS & MILESTONES

A MOTHER'S MEMOIR OF LOVE & LEGACY

DESCRIBE THE FIRST TIME YOU HELD YOUR CHILD

WHAT DETAILS MAKE IT VIVID?

WHAT SMALL MILESTONES FELT UNEXPECTEDLY MEANINGFUL?

HOW DID YOU CHOOSE YOUR CHILD'S NAME?

WHAT ROUTINES HELPED YOU SETTLE INTO LIFE WITH A NEW BABY OR CHILD?

WHAT PHOTOS OR KEEPSAKES FROM THE EARLY YEARS STILL MOVE YOU?

_____
_____
_____
_____
_____
_____
_____
_____
_____
_____

DESCRIBE A BEDTIME, FEEDING, OR MORNING ROUTINE THAT FELT SACRED.

_____
_____
_____
_____
_____
_____
_____
_____
_____
_____

WHAT WAS A FAVORITE 'FIRST' —FIRST SMILE, WORD, STEP, OR DAY OF SCHOOL?

HOW DID YOU DOCUMENT YOUR CHILD'S GROWTH ?

HOW DID YOU DOCUMENT YOUR CHILD'S STORIES?

WHAT DID AN ORDINARY DAY LOOK LIKE IN THE EARLY YEARS?

WHAT WAS A HARD MILESTONE THAT YOU GREW THROUGH TOGETHER?

additional notes

additional notes

Capture the Moments

Add photos or draw pictures that represent this chapter of your life.

Memories

Memories

Memories

> "IN EVERY CONCEIVABLE MANNER, THE FAMILY IS THE LINK TO OUR PAST, BRIDGE TO OUR FUTURE."
> — ALEX HALEY

CARRIED IN MY HEART

DAILY LIFE & ROUTINES

A MOTHER'S MEMOIR OF LOVE & LEGACY

WHAT DOES A WEEKDAY LOOK LIKE FOR YOUR FAMILY—MORNING TO NIGHT?

HOW DO YOU SHARE RESPONSIBILITIES AT HOME?

WHAT MAKES YOUR HOUSEHOLD RUN SMOOTHLY (MOST DAYS)?

WHAT SMALL ROUTINES CONNECT YOU WITH YOUR CHILD EACH DAY?

HOW DO YOU CARVE OUT ONE-ON-ONE TIME WITH YOUR CHILD?

DESCRIBE A TYPICAL WEEKEND—
WHAT DO YOU LOOK FORWARD TO?

WHAT IS A SMALL, ORDINARY MOMENT THAT YOU NEVER WANT TO FORGET?

THE BIGGEST?

WHAT IS YOUR APPROACH TO SCREENS, PLAY, AND LEARNING AT HOME?

HOW DO YOU HANDLE CHORES, ALLOWANCES, OR RESPONSIBILITIES?

HOW DO YOU CELEBRATE TINY WINS IN EVERYDAY LIFE?

additional notes

additional notes

Capture the Moments

Add photos or draw pictures that represent this chapter of your life.

Memories

Memories

Memories

"WE ARE SHAPED AND FASHIONED BY WHAT WE LOVE."
— JOHANN WOLFGANG VON GOETHE

CARRIED IN MY HEART

LOVE, JOY & HUMOR

A MOTHER'S MEMOIR OF LOVE & LEGACY

WHAT IS A MEMORY THAT STILL MAKES YOU LAUGH?

WHY?

WHAT MOMENTS WITH YOUR CHILD FEEL LIKE PURE JOY?

HOW DO YOU SHOW LOVE IN WAYS YOUR CHILD UNDERSTANDS?

WHAT'S A SILLY TRADITION YOU SHARE THAT ALWAYS BRINGS SMILES?

WHAT IS YOUR CHILD'S SENSE OF HUMOR LIKE?

YOURS AS A MOTHER?

WHEN DID YOUR CHILD COMFORT YOU?

HOW DID THAT FEEL?

HOW DO YOU MAKE ORDINARY DAYS FEEL SPECIAL?

DESCRIBE A JOYFUL SURPRISE YOUR CHILD GAVE YOU.

WHAT MUSIC, STORIES, OR JOKES ARE PART OF YOUR FAMILY'S FUN?

WHAT ARE THREE SMALL THINGS ABOUT YOUR CHILD YOU LOVE NOTICING RIGHT NOW?

additional notes

additional notes

Capture the Moments

Add photos or draw pictures that represent this chapter of your life.

Memories

Memories

Memories

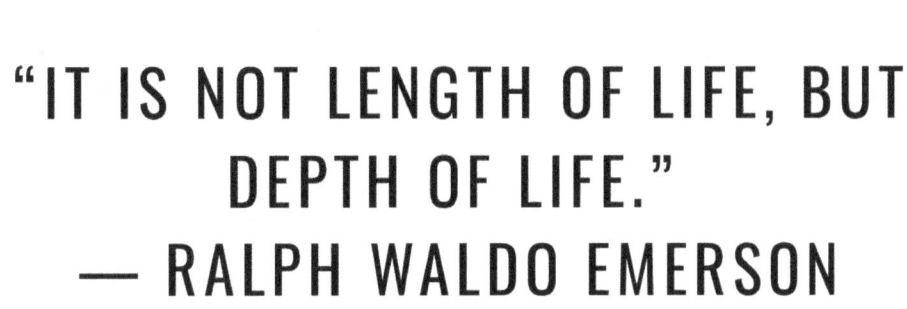

A MOTHER'S MEMOIR OF LOVE & LEGACY

CARRIED IN MY HEART

CHALLENGES & RESILIENCE

A MOTHER'S MEMOIR OF LOVE & LEGACY

WHAT BOUNDARIES PROTECT YOUR FAMILY'S WELLBEING?

HOW DO YOU REPAIR AFTER CONFLICT?

WITH YOUR CHILD OR CO-PARENT?

DESCRIBE A TIME YOU ADVOCATED FOR YOUR CHILD

WHAT DID YOU LEARN?

HOW DO YOU CARE FOR YOURSELF SO YOU CAN CARE FOR YOUR CHILD?

WHAT DID YOU LET GO OF TO MAKE ROOM FOR WHAT MATTERS MOST?

WHAT HAS BEEN ONE OF YOUR HARDEST MOMENTS AS A MOTHER, AND HOW DID YOU GET THROUGH IT?

WHAT ROLE DOES YOUR SUPPORT SYSTEM PLAY IN TOUGH SEASONS?

___

HOW DO YOU TEACH PERSEVERANCE BY EXAMPLE?

___

WHEN DID YOU CHANGE YOUR MIND OR APPROACH?

WHY?

HOW DO YOU HANDLE WORRY ABOUT YOUR CHILD'S HEALTH, LEARNING, OR FRIENDSHIPS?

additional notes

additional notes

Capture the Moments

Add photos or draw pictures that represent this chapter of your life.

Memories

Memories

> "LIFE CAN ONLY BE UNDERSTOOD BACKWARDS; BUT IT MUST BE LIVED FORWARDS."
> — SØREN KIERKEGAARD

A MOTHER'S MEMOIR OF LOVE & LEGACY

CARRIED IN MY HEART

VALUES, FAITH & CHARACTER

A MOTHER'S MEMOIR OF LOVE & LEGACY

WHICH VALUES GUIDE YOUR PARENTING MOST STRONGLY?

WHAT STORIES, BOOKS, OR QUOTES DO YOU USE TO TEACH CHARACTER?

WHAT SPIRITUAL, FAITH, OR PHILOSOPHICAL PRACTICES SHAPE YOUR HOME?

HOW DO YOU CULTIVATE GRATITUDE AS A FAMILY?

HOW DID YOU BEGIN?

HOW DO YOU TALK ABOUT KINDNESS, FAIRNESS, AND INTEGRITY AT HOME?

HOW DO YOU MODEL APOLOGY, REPAIR, AND FORGIVENESS?

HOW DO YOU HELP YOUR CHILD FIND THEIR VOICE AND BOUNDARIES?

WHAT CONVERSATIONS HAVE YOU HAD ABOUT IDENTITY, CULTURE, OR JUSTICE?

WHAT RULES OR EXPECTATIONS MATTER?

WHY THOSE?

WHAT DOES COURAGE LOOK LIKE IN YOUR FAMILY?

additional notes

additional notes

Capture the Moments

Add photos or draw pictures that represent this chapter of your life.

Memories

Memories

> "THE MEANING OF LIFE IS TO FIND YOUR GIFT. THE PURPOSE OF LIFE IS TO GIVE IT AWAY."
> — PABLO PICASSO

CARRIED IN MY HEART

TRADITIONS & FAMILY CULTURE

A MOTHER'S MEMOIR OF LOVE & LEGACY

WHAT FAMILY TRADITIONS DID YOU INHERIT?

WHICH HAVE YOU CREATED?

HOW DO YOU CELEBRATE BIRTHDAYS, HOLIDAYS, OR MILESTONES?

WHAT FOODS, SONGS, OR STORIES DEFINE YOUR FAMILY'S CULTURE?

WHAT IS A WEEKLY RITUAL YOU LOVE (GAME NIGHT, MOVIE NIGHT, ETC.)?

HOW DO YOU KEEP EXTENDED FAMILY CONNECTED ACROSS DISTANCE OR TIME?

WHAT OBJECTS IN YOUR HOME HOLD FAMILY MEANING?

HOW DO YOU HONOR ANCESTORS OR THE PEOPLE WHO CAME BEFORE YOU?

WHAT TRAVEL OR SEASONAL TRADITIONS DO YOU CHERISH?

WHAT ROUTINES HELP YOU THROUGH TRANSITIONS AND GOODBYES?

WHY?

HOW DO YOU WANT YOUR FAMILY CULTURE TO EVOLVE AS YOUR CHILD GROWS?

additional notes

additional notes

Capture the Moments

Add photos or draw pictures that represent this chapter of your life.

Memories

Memories

Memories

> "THE GREATEST USE OF LIFE IS TO SPEND IT FOR SOMETHING THAT WILL OUTLAST IT."
> — WILLIAM JAMES

A MOTHER'S MEMOIR OF LOVE & LEGACY

CARRIED IN MY HEART

WORK, TIME & BALANCE

A MOTHER'S MEMOIR OF LOVE & LEGACY

HOW DO YOU BALANCE WORK AND FAMILY?

WHAT HAS CHANGED OVER TIME?

WHAT SUPPORT (FORMAL OR INFORMAL) HELPS YOU MANAGE RESPONSIBILITIES?

HOW DO YOU HANDLE GUILT OR PRESSURE AROUND COMPETING PRIORITIES?

WHAT ROUTINES PROTECT REST AND PLAY FOR YOUR FAMILY?

HOW DO YOU STAY CONNECTED WITH YOUR CHILD DURING BUSY SEASONS?

WHAT BOUNDARIES OR SYSTEMS AT WORK HELP YOU BE PRESENT AT HOME?

WHY?

HOW DO YOU MANAGE FINANCES IN WAYS THAT REFLECT YOUR VALUES?

WHAT DID YOU LEARN FROM A SEASON OF BURNOUT OR OVERWHELM?

WHAT WOULD YOUR IDEAL WEEK LOOK LIKE, AND WHAT SMALL STEPS MOVE YOU CLOSER?

HOW DO YOU PLAN FOR CHILDCARE, SCHOOL, OR ACTIVITIES AS NEEDS CHANGE?

additional notes

additional notes

Capture the Moments

Add photos or draw pictures that represent this chapter of your life.

Memories

Memories

Memories

> "THE GREATEST THING YOU'LL EVER LEARN IS JUST TO LOVE AND BE LOVED IN RETURN."
> — EDEN AHBEZ

THE LIGHT THAT LINGERS

LESSONS, GUIDANCE & ADVICE

A MOTHER'S MEMOIR OF LOVE & LEGACY

WHAT'S ONE LESSON YOU RETURN TO AGAIN AND AGAIN WITH YOUR CHILD?

HOW DO YOU TEACH YOUR CHILD ABOUT FRIENDSHIP AND EMPATHY?

WHAT DO YOU HOPE YOUR CHILD LEARNS ABOUT FAILURE AND TRYING AGAIN?

HOW DO YOU ENCOURAGE CREATIVITY AND CURIOSITY AT HOME?

WHY IS THIS IMPORTANT?

WHAT MONEY, WORK, OR LIFE SKILLS DO YOU WANT TO PASS ON?

HOW DO YOU TALK ABOUT DIGITAL LIFE— PRIVACY, KINDNESS, AND BALANCE?

WHAT STORIES FROM YOUR OWN LIFE DO YOU SHARE TO TEACH WISDOM?

HOW DO YOU HELP YOUR CHILD NOTICE AND GROW THEIR STRENGTHS?

WHAT IS ADVICE YOU WOULD WRITE TO YOUR CHILD FOR A FUTURE MILESTONE?

additional notes

additional notes

Capture the Moments

Add photos or draw pictures that represent this chapter of your life.

Memories

Memories

Memories

"OUR MOST TREASURED FAMILY HEIRLOOMS ARE OUR SWEET FAMILY MEMORIES."
— ANON

A MOTHER'S MEMOIR OF LOVE & LEGACY

CARRIED IN MY HEART

LEGACY & DREAMS FOR MY CHILD

A MOTHER'S MEMOIR OF LOVE & LEGACY

WHAT DO YOU WANT YOUR CHILD TO REMEMBER MOST ABOUT GROWING UP WITH YOU?

WHAT ARE YOUR HOPES FOR YOUR CHILD'S CHARACTER AND HAPPINESS?

HOW DO YOU WANT YOUR CHILD TO EXPERIENCE LOVE AND SAFETY IN YOUR HOME?

WHAT KIND OF WORLD DO YOU HOPE YOUR CHILD INHERITS—AND HOW DO YOU HELP BUILD IT?

WHAT LETTERS OR MESSAGES WOULD YOU LEAVE FOR FUTURE MILESTONES?

WHICH FAMILY STORIES DO YOU MOST WANT TO PASS ALONG?

WHAT KEEPSAKES SHOULD YOUR CHILD HAVE ONE DAY—AND WHY?

WHAT PROMISE DO YOU WANT TO MAKE TO YOUR CHILD AND KEEP?

HOW DO YOU WANT TO BE REMEMBERED AS A MOTHER?

IF YOUR CHILD READS THIS MEMOIR YEARS FROM NOW, WHAT WOULD YOU LIKE TO SAY TO THEM?

additional notes

additional notes

Capture the Moments

Add photos or draw pictures that represent this chapter of your life.

Memories

Memories

> "OWNING OUR STORY AND LOVING OURSELVES THROUGH THAT PROCESS IS THE BRAVEST THING WE'LL EVER DO."
> — BRENÉ BROWN

A MOTHER'S MEMOIR OF LOVE & LEGACY

Life's *Reflections*

(Overview)
SUMMARIZE KEY EVENTS

(Achievements)
WHAT WERE YOUR MAJOR ACHIEVEMENTS?

(Gratitude)
LIST THREE THINGS YOU'RE MOST GRATEFUL FOR.

(Priorities)
IDENTIFY KEY PRIORITIES AND GOALS.

- ○ _____
- ○ _____
- ○ _____
- ○ _____
- ○ _____

A MOTHER'S MEMOIR OF LOVE & LEGACY

Dear _____,
Letter to Loved One

_____
_____
_____
_____
_____
_____
_____
_____
_____
_____
_____
_____
_____
_____
_____
_____
_____
_____
_____

WITH LOVE,

_____

Letter to Loved One

Dear _____ ,

_____
_____
_____
_____
_____
_____
_____
_____
_____
_____
_____
_____
_____
_____
_____
_____
_____
_____
_____
_____
_____

With Love,

_____

LETTER TO LOVED ONE

Dear _____,

_____
_____
_____
_____
_____
_____
_____
_____
_____
_____
_____
_____
_____
_____
_____
_____
_____
_____
_____
_____
_____
_____

WITH LOVE,
_____

Dear _____,

LETTER TO LOVED ONE

WITH LOVE,

*D*EAR LETTER TO LOVED ONE

_____ ,

WITH LOVE,

_____

Capture the Moments

Add photos or draw pictures that represent this chapter of your life.

Memories

Memories

Memories

Capture the Moments

Add photos or draw pictures that represent this chapter of your life.

Memories

Memories

"YOUR STORY IS WHAT YOU HAVE, WHAT YOU WILL ALWAYS HAVE. IT IS SOMETHING TO OWN."
— MICHELLE OBAMA

ADDITIONAL MEMOIR PUBLICATIONS

ROOTED IN YOU
A CHILD'S MEMOIR OF LOVE AND GRATITUDE

THE LIGHT THAT LINGERS
A PERSONAL MEMOIR OF LOVE AND LIFE

GUIDED BY MY HANDS
A FATHER'S MEMOIR OF LOVE AND STRENGTH

BOUND BY OUR VOWS
A SPOUSE'S MEMOIR OF LOVE AND DEVOTION

FOR MORE INFORMATION OR
TO PURCHASE ADDITIONAL COPIES
WWW.ATOSHALOGAN.COM

Every life tells a story...

A mother's story is more than a record of events—it is a legacy of love, sacrifice, and strength. In these pages, a mother reflects on the joys and challenges of nurturing life, offering wisdom that transcends generations. This memoir is both a tribute and a treasure, reminding readers that a mother's influence is timeless and her love, everlasting.

More than a record of one life, this memoir is an invitation to reflect on your own story. It is a reminder that while we cannot choose every circumstance, we can choose the legacy we leave behind.

Whether you are seeking encouragement, reflection, or simply a heartfelt story, this book offers something to carry with you. May it inspire you to embrace your own journey with gratitude, courage, and love.

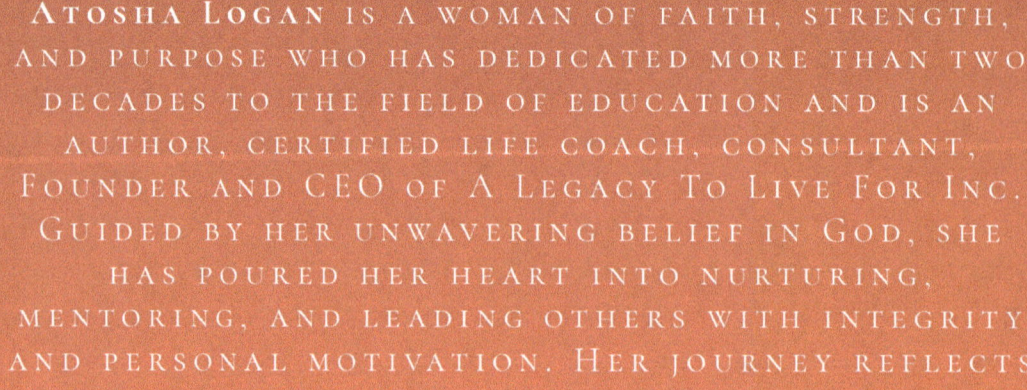

Atosha Logan is a woman of faith, strength, and purpose who has dedicated more than two decades to the field of education and is an author, certified life coach, consultant, Founder and CEO of A Legacy To Live For Inc. Guided by her unwavering belief in God, she has poured her heart into nurturing, mentoring, and leading others with integrity and personal motivation. Her journey reflects resilience, hope, and a deep commitment to uplifting and empowering others.

www.ingramcontent.com/pod-product-compliance
Lightning Source LLC
Chambersburg PA
CBHW081357070526
44583CB00020B/2587